Maggie McLeod, a native Scot, living in Edinburgh, is a professional Scottish tourist guide (Blue Badge). Blue Badge guides are the official accredited tourist guides recognised by Scottish government and Visit Scotland.

Maggie has a certificate in Scottish studies from the University of Edinburgh, holds a diploma in Wines & Spirits and is a Scotch Whisky ambassador.

Maggie has travelled extensively throughout Scotland guiding individuals and small groups over the last 20 years but the islands have always been her passion.

To my lovely grandchildren who have always inspired me,
Maia, Elsie, Naomi and Keir.

Maggie McLeod

ISLAY AND ITS WHISKIES

The ONLY Islay Guidebook you need

AUSTIN MACAULEY PUBLISHERS™

LONDON • CAMBRIDGE • NEW YORK • SHARJAH

A CIP catalogue record for this title is available from the British Library.

ISBN 9781398421073 (Paperback)
ISBN 9781398421080 (ePub e-book)

www.austinmacauley.com

First Published 2023
Austin Macauley Publishers Ltd®
1 Canada Square
Canary Wharf
London
E14 5AA

To my colleague and good friend, Ronnie Berri. Ronnie is a Scottish tourist guide, a well-known whisky expert and keeper of the Quaich.

NB: The Keepers is an exclusive and international society that recognises those that have shown outstanding commitment to the Scotch whisky industry.

My grateful thanks to him for the insider tips and information on Islay's famous distilleries, and for sharing some of his excellent photographs.

Table of Contents

Foreword

This pocket guidebook is all you need to enhance your Islay visit. It is the ideal companion for the Scotch Whisky dreamers and those who share a passion for Scotland's islands.

Scotch Whisky producers are rightly proud of their whiskies. They would like you to enjoy them by drinking responsibly.

www.drinkaware.co.uk

Use a designated driver.

Background

The Inner Hebridean Island of Islay (*pronounced Aye la*) is surrounded by sea, steeped in history, and immersed in Whisky.

Islay is also known as the Happy Isle, perhaps due to the longevity of the islanders or the nine (currently), fine Malt Whisky Distilleries dispersed throughout the Island. Islay certainly punches above her weight economically as she provides ¼ of Scotland's Malt Whisky exports.

Islay is approximately 25 miles from north to south and 14 miles from east to west with a population of around 3,500 Ileachs. An Ileach really refers to those born on the Island, however, many inhabitants are not Islay-born but have chosen to make their home there. Islay is very fertile island, aka the "Queen of the Hebrides". This is probably the reason the Lords of the Isles (more on them later) chose it for their power base in the Middle Ages. Islay's other industries are agriculture and tourism.

'Uisge beatha' or Whisky is believed to have started almost 800 years ago when Agnes, daughter of a Baron of Ulster, accompanied by a physician named Macbeth, came to marry Angus Og (Lord of the Isles). Among their possessions, they brought a recipe for the Water of Life, and the rest, they say, is history…

Ptolomy (AD 127–145) said the island was famous for horses. An old Gaelic proverb says, "an Islay man would carry a saddle and bridle for 1½ miles to ride for half a mile". Certainly, the Islay surname MacEachran originates from a person who was skilled in the riding of horses or who owned many horses. The Gaelic form of the name was MacEachthighearna, try saying that after a dram or two of fine Islay Malt! This translates as "son of the horse-lord". This surname is still to be found on Islay.

(Caol Isla Distillery)

Islay is a bird watcher's paradise. Along the glorious 130-mile coastline, you can find seals, otters, wading birds, oystercatchers, gannets, terns, gulls, ducks, shags, cormorants, etc. Farmlands are home to lapwings, curlews, corncrakes, rare choughs, and around fifty thousand wild geese who spend their winters here.

In addition, Buzzards, Hen Harriers, Golden Eagles, White Tailed Sea Eagles, and other birds of prey can also be seen. Dolphins and basking sharks are often spotted from the coastal areas or from a boat or ferry. Otters are shy and not easy to see, but your best chances are on Caol Ila beach and north of Bunnahabhain. Red deer, Roe Deer, Fallow Deer, and brown hare are also common.

Weather

In common with Scotland's west coast, Islay's climate benefits from the warm Gulf Stream, bringing cool winters with little frost or snow and mild summers. The driest, most pleasant weather, on average, is from April to July when rainfall is less than in other months. November to February are the wettest and windiest months, and there are crisp winter days and snowfall, especially on higher grounds.

Getting there

Ferry: Many visitors arrive by daily ferry from Kennacraig on the Scottish mainland (1 hour 55 mins crossing time) or once weekly from Oban. The ferry arrives at either

Port Askaig or Port Ellen. Visit the CalMac website for information. www.calmac.co.uk

Fly: You can also fly to Islay (45 mins from Glasgow) with Loganair operating flights from Edinburgh and Glasgow and Hebridean Air Services running flights from Colonsay and Oban. www.loganair.co.uk

Bus: From Glasgow, Buchanan Street Bus Station, there is a city link coach which takes you to the ferry port at Kennacraig four times every day. www.citylink.co.uk

Car: Self-drive from the major cities of Edinburgh or Glasgow to the Ferry Terminal at Kennacraig (allow 2 hours 45 mins from Glasgow to Kennacraig).

Remember to use a designated driver if you intend to sample the famous whisky. Scotland has a very strict policy on drink driving.

Accommodation: A wide range of accommodation is on offer. www.islayjura.com

Tour Suggestion 1:
Bowmore and
Port Ellen Distilleries

This guidebook book tells you how to get the best out of your time on Islay. Some suggested tour routes are featured to ensure you don't miss anything of interest.

Bowmore is Islay's admin capital and main shopping centre. Bowmore was planned in the 1760s by Daniel Campbell the Laird of Islay House. The inhabitants of the original village were cleared from the land around the Laird's grand summer residence. A tiny cemetery south of Islay House is the only reminder of the old village.

This story is not uncommon as the same event happened in Inveraray when the Duke of Argyll wanted a distance between himself and his tenants. These new planned villages of Bowmore and Inveraray were well-designed attractive small towns, probably a big improvement on how the locals had lived before, although there is no one is alive today who can testify, the layout of these two towns have much in common.

The establishment of planned villages in Scotland was part of the general reorganisation of estates which occurred in the period of agricultural "improvement". They were necessary as centres for rural industry and also to absorb the population displaced from the land as a result of the Highland clearances. 130 such villages were founded between 1770–1830 but very few in Highlands and Islands.

When visiting Bowmore, don't miss out on **Kilarrow Round Church** (1767). This Church dominates the town. Walk into the graveyard and look for the grave of Islay-born hero "Tartan Pimpernel". Dr Donald Caskie aka "Tartan Pimpernel" was Minister of the Scots Kirk in Paris during World War 2. When Paris was invaded, he provided an escape route for up to 500 Allied soldiers, sailors, and airmen. He was later awarded the OBE. Dr Caskie was born in Bowmore in 1902.

The locals will tell you that the round design of the Church is because "devil canna lurk in corners"[1].

Inside the church, you will see two sarcophagi. In one sarcophagus lies the first wife of the Laird, Mr Campbell. Mr Campbell later remarried a French lady who forbade his body to lie beside his first wife when he died. Hence, he was laid to rest in the lobby alongside their two-year-old son.

---

[1] The devil cannot hide in corners.

(Bowmore graveyard)

Bowmore Distillery (*meaning: Big Cow*) – The oldest Distillery on Islay. Established in 1779 by a local merchant, John P Simpson. The distillery overlooks Loch Indaal, rich in seafowl, gulls, ducks, waders. You will notice that all the distilleries in Islay face the sea with their own pier and their name clearly visible. Essential when all necessary supplies come from ships, see info on Steam Puffers below.

Now owned by Morrison Bowmore Distillers Ltd, a holding company owned by Japanese drinks company, Beam Suntory with a capacity for two Million Litres. Bowmore has a unique onion-shaped pagoda roof and proudly owns the oldest existing maturation warehouse in Scotland, Vault No 1, dating from 1779. Part of the warehouse walls lies below sea level.

The peat level in the malt, both the 30% malt from their own malting floor and the remaining 70%, is 25ppm, which ensures Bowmore is considerably less smoky than their neighbours, the Kildalton coast monsters!

A recent successful bottling launched in 2013 was named "The Devil`s Cask" recounting a local story of the Devil being chased from the round Church in the centre of Bowmore to the harbour. The Devil finally escaping Islay in a Bowmore whisky cask aboard an old steam puffer[2].

---

[2] A Steam Puffer is a small coal-fired and single-masted cargo ship, which provided a vital supply link around Scotland's west coast. Their flat bottoms allowed them to beach and unload at low tide.

Bowmore is often regarded as a luxury malt, more lightly peated than others, therefore more approachable to drinkers. Often found in Travel retailers with enticing bottle shapes and packaging.

Possibly the nicest place to enjoy a dram or two is Bowmore's tempting tasting bar. Large windows and a balcony offer stunning views across Loch Indaal to the Rhinns of Islay and the distillery buildings of Bruichladdich on the opposite shore. A small display tells Bowmore's history, the centrepiece of which is a unique bottle of 50-year-old Bowmore. Some visitors hope to find the legendary bottling of the Black Bowmore from 1964. Unfortunately, they are disappointed as these can only be found in private collections or auctions where a bottle can set you back to £12–15,000 or more!

Bowmore's standard range consists of the No 1 named after their oldest warehouse. There are 12 years old, 15, 18, and 25 years old. Occasionally, on offer is the opportunity to hand fill your bottles direct from casks. Also, at the distillery shop visitors can purchase a range of distillery exclusives or special bottlings.

The Bowmore malt style/character is rich and full with citrus overtones and notes of cocoa. A very complex finish of chocolate mixed with a sweet note. Try it yourself with a bar of good quality dark chocolate!

The Morrison **Bowmore** Distillery and MacTaggart family plus fundraising efforts of locals were successful in funding a new swimming pool in 1993. The "Mactaggart

---

Ideal for supplying barley and other essentials and shipping out whisky casks to the mainland for bottling and onward travel.

Centre" is an award-winning building and very innovative as distillery "waste" heat is used to heat the pool which is housed in an old distillery warehouse.

Bowmore can also offer accommodation in restored 4* Distillery cottages.

Explore the south side of the Island, this combines peat, distilleries, ancient crosses, and stunning seascape.

(Paps of Jura)

Peat, an essential ingredient

Leaving Bowmore and head to the high road, this is the older road on Islay running on the higher ground almost parallel to the main Airport road, you can reach it from the central village of Bowmore by taking a smaller road behind the Round Church on the right.

On reaching the High Road, turn right and almost immediately you will come across new and old [3]peat cutting

---

[3] Peatlands occur in poorly drained areas that experience high rainfall, leading to accumulation of undecayed plant material, hence peat formation. Blanket Bog is very scarce globally but occurs in N and W Scotland. Fluffy white heads of bog cotton often signify

banks, the best time to view fresh peat cutting is from late April to June or July.

Look to the left for the large brown sheds in the far distance, this is Castlehill peat moss, this peat is used by Port Ellen maltings, c2,000 tonnes are mechanically cut each year by the "sausage machine", a cutting device dragged behind a tractor which cuts the peat into sausage-like shapes.

Local people cut small amounts by hand for domestic use, their peats can be seen drying next to deep cutting banks or bagged ready to be moved. Islanders cut between half a tonne to a tonne each and will choose the deeper, darker lying peat. This older peat gives out more heat and less smoke, the

(Peat beds)

reverse is true for the distilleries who prefer the upper layers, which are not yet fully decomposed and produce more smoke to flavour the drying barley. You might see cutting taking place, usually at weekends.

Peat from Islay imparts smoky peaty notes of iodine, antiseptic, and TCP, familiar in many of the Islay whiskies. This is probably due to the seaweed which forms the decomposing plant material. There's no definite explanation or proof, but this is a commonly held belief explaining the unique Islay

---

bogs. Seen at Duich Moss and Watershed Moss on the Rhinns of Islay.

reek[4]. By contrast peat cut in mainland Scotland, e.g., Speyside and Highland imparts more earthy and stale tobacco notes.

Continue on the high road (B8016) towards the village of Port Ellen passing by the large Port Ellen Maltings, the highest building on the island dating from 1974. Owned by the giant drinks company, Diageo. Up to 1,500 tonnes of barley arrive at Port Ellen every two weeks by a special grain boat. One tonne produces 415–420 litres of alcohol. Then the malted barley finds its way to some of the island distilleries, currently, **Bowmore, Laphroaig,** and sometimes **Bunnahabhain.**

Port Ellen Distillery

Tucked away, behind the tall Malting structure is the soon-to-be-reopened and much anticipated. The double Doig pagoda chimneys and extractor fans still tower above the old site. This distillery ceased production in 1983, finally closing its doors in 1987. The current building forms part of Diageo's recent £35m investment to reopen the distillery along with Brora in the Northern Highlands. Work began in late 2019 and the newly reopened **Port Ellen** is scheduled to begin production in 2022.

Port Ellen was a legendary malt, loved by many "peat freaks" and is regarded as one of the finest Islay Malts to be had – if you can afford it!

The town of **Port Ellen** was founded by 4th Laird, Walter Campbell in 1821 and named for his wife. This is

---

[4] Reek is a Scottish word meaning odour or smell.

the main ferry terminal for heavy freight, the other ferry terminal being Port Askaig.

Walkers and hikers: Try the recently completed path from Port Ellen to Ardbeg (approx. 3 miles / 5 km) and named for the three distillery villages on its route – "Three Distilleries Pathway". (**Laphroaig, Lagavulin, and Ardbeg**)

Apart from a small section at Lagavulin, it is off-road, running parallel with the A846. The surface is excellent for both walking and cycling. It would also be suitable for wheelchairs/strollers but be warned, the path is undulating, particularly towards either end, with a couple of short steep sections.

There is a delightful variety of scenery and wildlife along the way. Buzzards are common, deer graze in adjacent woods. A detour to the shore behind Lagavulin Distillery and, if you approach quietly, you could spot otters. There is also access from the path to the monument to Alexander McDougall at Laphroaig and the ruins of Dùn Naomhaig (Dunyvaig) castle at Lagavulin.

For vehicles: Continue on A846 and just outside Port Ellen is one of Islay's standing stones, to view, take a slight detour and turn left onto a little road and after a few hundred metres a solitary standing stone erected c 4,000 years ago comes into view.

Back on the main road, on the right, is a small hill with a memorial on top commemorating an Islay man, General Alexander McDougall, born in this area in 1732 and considered a hero in the US Revolutionary War. He emigrated to the USA with his family and fought alongside other colonials for liberty against the British. He enjoyed a long and illustrious career becoming President of the First Bank in the State of New York also serving in the Senate. There is MacDougall (*sic*) Street in Manhattan and a memorial in Greenwich Village on the wall of the First Presbyterian Church of New York.Look out as we pass three great distilleries, each sitting by their private bays and jetties where the grain comes in and whisky goes out. Above, in the hills on left, are the lochs which feed each one, all arranged like a line of bowls on a shelf.

Tour Suggestion 2:
Laphroaig, Lagavulin
and Ardbeg Distilleries

Celtic Christianity

Before we indulge the whisky geeks, some ancient history awaits. Continue on this road to see one of the finest early High Crosses in Great Britain c800AD. The 2.65m **Kildalton Cross** stands outside the ancient Chapel of Kildalton. The Chapel dates from 12th/13th C.

Kildalton *(Cill Daltan)* – Church of the foster child or disciple, perhaps referring to St John the Evangelist "beloved disciple". There is no evidence of a Saint called Daltan anywhere in the Celtic world. This cross is considered to be one of the finest early crosses in GB.

By the north door of the chapel is a stoup (basin for holy water) which never runs out even in the driest season. Check it for yourself. The Chapel Loft area probably had accommodation for the cleric who would have access via a ladder by a wooden screen separating the chancel or altar area from the Nave. In the recesses of the doors, you can see evidence of heavy drawbars. Sadly, the Chapel has been subject to stone robbing over the years.

The Cross is made from local greenstone (Dalradian metamorphosed lava) a very hard rock resistant to weathering.

(Kildalton Cross)

In 1862, the Ramsays of Kildalton took down the cross as it was in danger of falling over, under the foundations they found a small cross and the remains of a man and woman who appeared to have died violently by the cruel method of spread-eagling often used by Vikings.

In the Museum of Islay Life in Port Charlotte, you can see a drawing, made in 1862, of the small cross found underneath.

There are some very fine medieval 15th C grave slabs, featuring warriors brandishing their doublehanded swords. These grave slabs are commonplace in Islay and throughout the West Highlands and Islands.

There is a replica of the Kildalton Cross in the National Museum of Scotland in Edinburgh. The Kildalton Cross is closely related to a group of three major High Crosses on Iona also dating from 8th C (St Oran's, St Martin's, and St John's).

The land adjacent to the chapel is known as the priest's field to this day, and there is another high cross, known as Thief's Cross (origin of name unknown), carved in different style and dating from 14/15th C.

It is said that St Columba (521–597AD) landed here from Iona and the cross was later placed as a sanctuary cross. If fugitives or criminals stayed for one year and one day they would be pardoned.

Laphroaig Distillery (Beautiful Hollow by Broad Bay)

Glasgow born, Bessie Williamson came to work as secretary to owner, Ian Hunter in 1934. Her aptitude saw her rapid promotion to Office Manager. When owner, Ian Hunter suffered a stroke in 1938, Bessie became Distillery Manager. During the war, distilleries were mothballed and Bessie was successful in preventing damage to stock and equipment whilst allowing the distillery to store over 400 tonnes of ammunition. Following Hunter's death, Bessie inherited the distillery and was instrumental in promoting the single Malt

Islay whisky to the US market. She enjoyed an illustrious career before she died in 1962.

(Dry Stone Cairn)

This cult whisky managed to beat the US prohibition laws (1920–1933) as it was imported legally as a "medicinal spirit". Reputed to be the favourite tipple of HM King Charles III. It has long held the No 1 spot among Islay malts in terms of sales and around 3.7 million bottles are sold annually. Owned by Beam Suntory Global Wine & Spirit. Laphroaig produces 3.3 million litres pa and has a 20% traditional malting floor.

Adjacent to the distillery is a field of small flags from many nations planted by "Friends of Laphroaig". Anyone can become a 'friend' online or by visiting the distillery, receive a certificate, own a 1 sq. ft plot of land here, and plant your flag.

On their next visit Friends receive a miniature as rent from the Distillery, this can only be claimed once yearly! There is a special bottling for the Annual May Festival "Cairdeas" meaning Friendship in Gaelic in tribute to their many Friends.

In the Visitor Centre are the books featuring the names of the early years 'friends'.

Look out for the bio centenary dry-stone cairn built to celebrate 200 years of the Distillery and officially 'opened' by then HRH Prince of Wales in 2015. There is a little locked door, I wonder what's inside?

Laphroaig's ten years old is the most sold expression of any Islay whisky but don't forget to try Laphroaig's ten-year-old Cask Strength. This is available as a distillery exclusive and completely different from the ten-year-old you may be familiar with. Be aware, cask strength is very strong, try it first then add a couple of drops of water to open the flavour.

Before you sample their famous Malts, enjoy a stroll along the narrow pier jutting into the sea for that perfect photograph of Laphroaig and admire the view to the tiny island of Texa.

Now abandoned, Texa is home to feral goats, otters, and seabirds. It is advisable to do this before your dram in case your balance is affected afterwards!

Lagavulin Distillery (Hollow of the Mill)

(Lagavulin)

After the '45[5] three brothers arrived, Ronald, Alex, Donald Johnston. Their sons started the distillery between 1810–16. Donald became the sole owner but died after falling

---

[5] The last Jacobite Uprising in 1745 led by Bonnie Prince Charlie

into an ale vat. His children were too young to inherit so the distillery was leased to Graham of Lagavulin, it is now owned by Diageo.

Over 2 million litres are produced annually, 95% of the spirit produced is sent by road to the mainland for filling and maturations at Blackgrange by Alloa and only around 16,000 casks are left to mature on Islay.

"*One-third genius, one-third megalomaniac and one-third eccentric;*" this quote refers to one of the pioneers of blended Scotch Whisky, Peter Mackie, aka Restless Peter. See his large portrait inside.

Mackie was born in 1855, he began working in the Glasgow-based family firm. He was sent to Lagavulin to learn the art of distillation. In 1891 the firm registered the White Horse brand as a blend with Lagavulin at its heart. It was named for White Horse Close in Edinburgh where the family had a long relationship with the Coaching Inn there. Following a dispute, he founded the Malt Mill Distillery within the Lagavulin site and poached staff from Laphroaig to work there. Malt Mill operated until 1960, one bottle from its final spirit run is still on display. Its maltings finally closed their doors in 1974 to make way for a new reception area for VIP visitors.

The lost distillery of Malt Mill and a mythical cask feature in Ken Loach's 2012 film *The Angels Share*.

Mackie enjoyed a long and tempestuous career and many stories abound, however, when it came to blending whisky, he was passionate about quality, using significant amounts of well-aged component malt whiskies, and he campaigned for a minimum age specification for Scotch whisky. He was a true Whisky Baron.

There are everchanging exclusive bottlings available at the distillery, in addition to their standard range. Recommended is the One-hour Cask Tasting Experience where six different Malts direct from the cask can be sampled. The Lagavulin style is a typical Islay malt with unique slightly tropical overtones, try them for yourself and see if you can detect pineapples.

Their famous eight-year-old is a recreation from a whisky first described in the 1880s by legendary whisky writer, Alfred Barnard, on his travels to Islay. His image and writing are featured prominently on the label.

Look out for the tombstone of Angus Johnston which hangs on the wall of the Distillery, his body was buried on Texa, but his grave slab didn't make it when the ship sank. The tombstone was recovered and is now a feature here. In the car park on the hillside is the old Distillery bell which was used to summon the workers to begin their day's work.

Whisky fans can ignore this – Behind the distillery on the headland is **Dunyvaig Castle**[6] don't let its present sorry condition fool you, in the past, this was a very large important military stronghold belonging to the Lordship of the Isles. Their political base can still be visited inland at Finlaggan on Islay, more on this later. Dunyvaig offered a safe anchorage for the fleet of Birlinns (galleys) belonging to the Lordship. There is a 17th C Tower, although the curtain wall is much earlier. A recent archaeological dig

---

[6] Dunyvaig was built by Donald or John Lord of the Isles, later captured by Macdonalds. When the castle was under attack, a piper played a warning tune, his right hand was later cut off as punishment.

unearthed numerous items of interest. It is possible to look around but, be aware, it has very uneven surfaces. Great views from the castle.

(Dunyvaig)

Car drivers: A slight diversion for a photo opportunity, pass the last house in Lagavulin village towards Ardbeg, turn right in a gap in stone wall crossing over the pathway, a small tarmac road leads you to the castle. Park at the last white house.

Ardbeg Distillery (Small Promontory)

The village was founded in 1815 by MacDougall of Ardbeg to house his distillery workers. They stopped malting their own barley in 1977 and the distillery was closed in 1981. After eight years it was reopened then closed again in 1996. Finally bought by Glenmorangie plc which, in turn, is owned by Moet Hennessy, LV, the French luxury goods company. The re-designed Ardbeg logo features a distinctive

Celtic A on a dark olive-green background and is globally recognised.

Ardbeg, at 55ppm of phenol in the malt, is perhaps the second most peated of all Islay malts after Bruichladdich's Octomore brand.

The "Committee" is the Ardbeg followers club, similar to Laphroaig, without the plot of land. Anyone can join and receive regular updates/news. Much anticipated, is the special bottling for the Festival, the "Committee" expression". This is offered at cask strength and attracts high prices in whisky auctions. A general release of the same bottling follows at an "easier" strength of 46% ABV and is more widely available.

The general releases of the distillery bottling range use local landmark names, e.g., Uigeadall (Loch Uigeadall is their water source), An Oa, Traigh Bhan, and Corryvreckan. Most whisky connoisseurs find these Gaelic names unpronounceable, great fun, and great marketing. Uigeadall has proved the most popular by aficionados. Extra Stills have been installed in the new Still House doubling the capacity to 2.4 million litres per year.

The Ardbeg Day during the festival in May is very entertaining and is celebrated by locals and whisky enthusiasts all over the world in specially dedicated pubs known as Ardbeg's Agencies. Expect fun, quirky activities, and different themes.

In 2011 Ardbeg organised an experiment to investigate how microgravity would affect the behaviour of terpenes, these are the building blocks of flavour for many foods, wines, and spirits.

A vial of whisky was sent to the International Space Station in a cargo spacecraft. Another vial of the same whisky was kept at the distillery for comparison.

The result was fascinating as the space samples were deemed "noticeably different" in terms of aroma and taste. The Old Kiln café/bistro here is recommended for local produce.

Tour Suggestion 3:
Caol Ila, Bunnahabhain, and Ardnahoe Distilleries

Depart Bowmore northwards.

Take the right fork A846 at Bridgend for a short distance to the **Islay Woollen Mill.**

This is a very picturesque working Mill with a wide range of products on sale. They have produced many Distillery tartans including the tartan for the Oscar-winning movie *Braveheart*. Products are available online or turn up and browse in the little shop.

Lords of the Isles: Before the next Whisky fix, explore some history and archaeology.

Continue northwards on A846 towards Ballygrant, the land around here is the Dunlossit Estate and was owned by Billionaire Banker, Bruno Shroder who died in 2019.

Lords of the Isles: Take a left turn towards **Finlagggan,** the domain of Lordship of the Isles (*Righ Innse Gall*). Two small islands in a loch were the power base of the Lordship. This dynasty began with Somerled, a Norse name meaning summer hunter/voyager. Celts and Norse had been intermarrying for centuries resulting in the term Gael/Gall. Many of the Clans in the NW Highlands share this mixed ancestral heritage.

On Eilean Mhor (*large island*) a body of 14 Clan Chiefs and the Lord had their administrative HQ/Parliament. The smaller island, linked by a causeway, was where the Council met. Their huge domain included the whole of Hebrides as well as large areas of mainland Scotland, particularly on the western seaboard and as far east as Ross and Inverness-shire. In 14th C it was virtually a separate Kingdom (a Sea Kingdom). Each clan had a hereditary role to play, lawyers, doctors, pipers, etc. Finlaggan was not fortified which indicates the security of the Lordship rule. Look out for Medieval warrior burial slabs.

The Lords ruled unchallenged, could muster thousands of fighting men, owned hundreds of longships (birlinns), and negotiated agreements with France, England, Ireland, and Scotland. Fighting platforms, extending from their Birlinns, were used to fend off their enemies demonstrating the sea was not a barrier. This way of life was destined not to last as they came under constant pressure from the Kings of Scotland to adopt feudal principles. Gradually it happened, and a feudal charter was granted, contrary to the Celtic prohibition of land ownership. Clan Chiefs became warlords rather than administrators. Finally, the end came in 1462 when John made a treaty with King Edward IV, leading to abolishing of title to the crown in 1493. It was followed by three centuries of feuding and strife. However, relationships between Chief and clan members sustained. The titular title "Lord of the Isles" is now held by HRH Prince Charles who proudly wears the Lordship tartan when visiting the north of Scotland.

(Finlaggan)

There is a small visitor centre with lots of good information. There are timber walkways and paths with Interpretation panels leading to the larger island (Eilean Mhor).

Depart Finlaggan and rejoin the main A846 towards Port Askaig and turn left towards Caol Isla.

Caol Ila Distillery (Kyle or strait of Islay)

Founded 1846 and currently owned by Diageo, hence, a sister distillery to Lagavulin. Port Ellen supplies the malted barley which is malted to a level of 35ppm.

Caol Ila is the largest distillery by capacity on the island currently producing 6.5 million litres of spirit every year. 15% of output is reserved for a single malt, while the remainder plays an important role in blending, most notably for Johnnie Walker Black Label and JW Double Black. However, you can find a small amount of Caol Ila malt in almost any blend within the Diageo portfolio and the spirit produced in Caol Ila is also used to trade with other companies for their blending processes.

Diageo also sells Caol Ila spirit to Cask Brokers and Independent bottlers (e.g., Gordon and MacPhail and Signatory vintage amongst others) to such an extent that one can find endless bottlings of Caol Ila available out with the standard range offers by Diageo.

Oddly enough, the location of Caol Ila is the most unlikely one on the island. There is a tricky approach to the site via a fairly steep narrow road. Don't forget, the location was chosen in 1846 when access was expected from the sea and not from land.

One of the best views of the neighbouring island of Jura and its famous Paps can be had from the distillery, especially the Stillhouse (see picture above). This can be viewed as part of the distillery tour.

The distillery has no active warehouses on-site, all Caol Ila spirit is driven by tanker truck tinkered away from the island every week for full maturation on the mainland, and not a drop of Caol Ila malt is matured on the island. Difficult to contemplate this while sampling their famous malt as it conveys all the esteemed qualities and character one would expect of an Islay Malt Whisky.

There is one old Warehouse on-site, out of use for many years, but now forms part of the upgrade to the Visitor Centre. When completed, a bar will be created and a footbridge to link the Visitor Centre and the Distillery.

The important role played by Caol Ila Malt in the Johnnie Walker brand is the reason this distillery was singled out by the parent company as one of the four pillars of the brand (the smoky note). The Visitor Centre upgrade here is working in tandem with the new Johnnie Walker Flagship Visitor Attraction in Edinburgh.

Caol Ila's special bottling for the 2019 Feis Ile Festival is a 22-year-old regarded by many as the finest of all amongst all the special festival bottlings for that year. Although not a very well-known brand, Caol Ila is highly respected by connoisseurs. For many years, the distillery also produced unpeated whisky, which was mainly sold to blenders, but now is proving very popular among connoisseurs.

Ardnahoe Distillery (Height of the Mound)

Production began here in Islay's newest distillery in November 2018. The distillery is set in a beautiful location between Caol Ila and Bunnahabhain on the stunning four-mile single-track road that connects them. It offers some of the best views of the Isle of Jura and the narrow sea channel (Kyle or Caol) between the islands.

The distillery is owned by the well-known Glasgow independent bottlers Hunter Laing. An agreement was reached with the Islay Estate of Lord Margadale (Morrison family) to build the Distillery and Visitor Centre alongside Loch Ardnahoe.

The Distillery offers a bistro café and whisky bar, the building is modern and blends well with the landscape. It is an environmentally friendly distillery featuring a decorative pagoda chimney roof. There is no malting on-site but malt arrives from the Port Ellen Maltings. Capacity, once full production is achieved, will be 1m litres of spirit per year, ranging from very lightly peated spirit at 5ppm to heavy peated at 40ppm. There is an attractive distillery shop where one can purchase or sample the full range of bottlings from the Hunter Laing range. These bottlings hail from many other whisky regions in Scotland making it an excellent whisky shop in its own right.

Interesting fact – the 1920s' Boby Malt Mill was brought from Fettercairn Distillery and the Stills Lyne Arms (part of the neck of the pot still connecting the still to the condenser) is the longest in Scotland at 7.5 metres. These condensers are unique on Islay as they use a traditional warm tub and not the more widely used Shell and Tube vertical condenser.

In 2017, the owners managed to convince the renowned, distiller Jim McEwan who had recently retired from Bruichladdich, to oversee the start of production and to help pinpoint the distillery spirit style for the future. He is now no longer involved.

Bunnahabhain Distillery (Foot of the River)

At the end of the single-track road passing Ardnahoe, this area offers amazing views of the famous Paps of Jura before reaching the most isolated of all Islay distilleries, Bunnahabhain.

At one time, the buildings surrounding this distillery were unattractive. However, much-needed changes have begun. Fifteen former worker's homes have been demolished, only two remain as part of a long-overdue upgrading. Four Warehouses and a new dedicated Visitor Centre has been constructed in addition to some necessary improvements in their production process.

This new phase will be more efficient and most of the spirit will now mature on the mainland. This is all due to the South African owners, Distell International, who bought the distillery in 2013.

'Bunna' (as it is affectionately known locally) is often regarded as the "hidden treasure" of Islay distilleries, unknown, unloved, and underappreciated as most visitors to the island do not make their way there. Don't make the same mistake!

Unusually for Islay, the 'Bunna' house style, or their main standard range, is extremely lightly peated, almost undetected at only 2ppm of smoke in the barley. The distillery also makes a standard range peated to a much higher level of 35 ppm, showing their versatility of production. They offer a wide variety of cask finishings, e.g., many dessert wines, Brandy, Sauternes, and Marsala alongside some varieties of sherries not commonly used, e.g. Fino, Manzanilla, and the excellent Palo Cortado and not forgetting the super sweet Pedro Ximenez.

Visitors have the opportunity to take the popular Warehouse 9 tour, where 4–5 casks will be open and a superb array of malts can be sampled directly from the casks. Other Islay distilleries offer a similar experience, however, the range on Bunnahabhain is truly inspiring and different.

After enjoying a dram, take a short coastline walk passing the former worker's cottages, through a gate, and out towards the projecting headland, you will spot the only shipwreck visible around the Islay coast. The rusty remains of the Wyre Majestic, a trawler wrecked in 1974, and now partly visible as it rests on the offshore rocks.

Tour Suggestion 4:
Kilchoman and
Bruichladdich Distilleries

Depart Bowmore, passing the old Fever Hospital now the Gaelic College overlooking the bay, through the village of Bridgend, where there is a good hotel and village store, rejoin the main A847 westwards. Passing a Victorian obelisk memorial to John Francis Campbell, a scholar, known to the Gaelic community as Iain Og. Just outside the village isthe Islay Estate with an interesting round tower built as an artillery battery during the Napoleonic Wars in the early 1800s.

This is the Estate of **Islay House**, a late 18th C grand mansion that has hosted many distinguished guests including HM the Queen and UK Prime Ministers. It was the original site of the long-gone Killarow Village demolished by the landlord when tenants were moved to the newly planned model village of Bowmore. Today, the grand star-star Islay House offers accommodation, fine dining, and events set in 28 acres overlooking Loch Indaal.

In the old stables yard, the former Home Farm which was once home to servants and workshops necessary to service

Islay House is now home to many artisan businesses. **Islay Square** has something for everyone. Islay Ales brewery, Nerabus Gin distillery, crafts, carpenters, quilter, photographers, etc. Don't miss it.

The original kitchen garden for the big house, dating from the 1700s, fell into disuse but has been successfully revived by local volunteers, growing vegetables, plants and supplying seasonal produce to the local community. The sundial in the centre is a remnant from the past. The garden is open all year and free to visit.

Leaving Islay Estate, continuing westwards, by the shore and near Black Rock is a Memorial plaque commemorating a Sunderland Flying boat that crashed during World War 2.

Continue on the A847, on the right passing a large flat expanse of grass, this is an example of a raised beach formed after the last Ice Age when glaciers retreated and the sea levels were much higher. Once upon a time, it was used as a nine-hole golf course but now is mainly for grazing sheep.

If you need a short break from your next whisky fix, aim northwards and follow the signs.

Continue north towards **Loch Gruinart RSPB Nature Reserve,** aka "Heathrow for geese" as 45% of the world's Barnacle geese fly in for winter. Endangered species are thriving here – snipe, corncrake, and chough, fortunately, Islay has no foxes, badgers, or squirrels to disturb them. The sheep and cattle belong to RSPB and farming are conducted in a wildlife-friendly way. Hay/silage is cut as late as possible to encourage the now globally threatened Corncrakes, the water levels are also controlled for wetland birds throughout the year.

Pop into the small Visitor Centre where there is lots more information available. If you are a bird fancier then make your way, on foot through woodland, to the bird hide with a viewing platform. Regular walks with the RSPB Rangers are on offer too, check website for details.

(Kilnave cross)

Continue northwards towards 12th C **Kilnave** Chapel. On the left, before you reach Kilnave lookout there is a ruined croft house with a black roof. This house is maintained by the RSPB as a nesting spot for rare choughs. If you are fortunate and visiting at the right time of year, you may see these distinctive black birds with red legs and beaks flying in and out. If you are in a small vehicle, open the gate and drive towards the Chapel, otherwise enjoy the short walk. Remember to close the gate afterwards.

Outside is early, rather eroded, High Cross from the Iona school of Carving and believed to date from c750AD. Over 8 ft high, much of the carving has flaked off, parts of the arms are missing too. The chapel is thought to date from 12th C and is named Cil Naoimh (Church of the Saint/Holy). The interior walls would have been plastered and most probably decorated. Pause at the entrance and turn the "Wishing Stone" three times clockwise. There are stunning views of the islands of Colonsay and Oronsay on a clear day.

In 1598 this was the scene of the bloody Battle of Traigh Gruinart between the Macdonalds of Islay and Macleans of Mull. As both sides were preparing for battle, a humpbacked hairy dwarf dubh sith) offered his services to Macleans as an archer. Macleans refused so he offered himself to MacDonalds who accepted.

Tradition says the dub sith (black fairy) climbed a tree and said he would deal with Clan Chief Maclean. It was a hot day and Lachlan MacLean stopped for a drink of water and took off his helmet, the dwarf aimed and fired. With their chief dead the clan lost the will to fight and took refuge in Kilnave Chapel. The MacDonalds retaliated by setting fire to the thatch roof, only one escaped by submerging himself in Loch Gruinart and breathing through a reed. The Cross was witness to these tragic events.

(Kilnave Chapel)

Continue northwards to Adnave, where you can enjoy a short stroll amongst the sand dunes. Take your binoculars and try to spot some rare bird visitors. On the left is Ardnave House and the very decorative building in a castle-style was a farm steading from the early 1800s.

The area around Ardnave was excavated and an extensive Bronze Age settlement was uncovered and many interesting artefacts were found. The site was recorded and finally reburied. Wonderful views to Nave Island.

Retrace your steps southwards towards the RSPB Reserve and turn left onto B8017. Look out for the Macdonald Castle on the island of Loch Gorm. There is a scenic circular route around the Loch.

This route will take you to **Kilchoman**.

Kilchoman Distillery (Church of Choman)

Kilchoman was set up in 2005, the first new distillery on Islay for 124 years. This venture was instigated by friends, Anthony Wills and Hamish French, a local farmer. (Hamish is no longer involved). The aim was to produce whisky in a traditional farm distillery way which was the norm until the late 1800s when commercialisation crept in. Kilchoman's Islay range is produced completely on-site, from barley to bottle and the distillery remains independent.

Since 2018 various works have been introduced to increase and improve production, e.g., a new malting floor and kiln, 30% of barley is now malted on-site, the remainder comes from Port Ellen, the barley is peated up to 50ppm. There is a new Still House which has increased capacity to 480,000 litres annually if needed. New warehousing to mature the spirit, a new bottling area, and last, but by no means least, a new Visitor Centre with a café/bistro.

The bold Islay style of malt now has legions of followers from around the world. This is remarkable considering that the distillery only produced 100,000 litres per year until 2017.

For single cask releases every year, the distillery uses Port, Muscatel, and varieties of sherry and other fortified wine casks. For their standard range, they mostly use ex-bourbon and Oloroso sherry casks.

Islay place name feature on their bottlings, e.g., Machir Bay (matured in American white oak), Sanaig, Loch Gorm (matured in Sherry cask, Coull Point and Saligo Bay).

Kilchoman is one of the very few whisky distilleries in Scotland that have their own small-scale bottling facility.

At one time every farm would grow grain to produce beer and whisky for their own needs. This encouraged the first levy by the Scottish Parliament in 1644. During the 1700s, at various times, whisky production was banned in order to save grain for food, especially during the years of poor harvests. However, many illegal Stills remained in operation and one old Still can be seen in the Museum of Islay Life at Port Charlotte.

Bruichladdich Distillery (Gentle slope of the sea)

Purpose-built 1881 around a square instead of growing haphazardly. In 2000, investors, some of whom are local estate owners, revived the distillery at a cost of £7m. Later, in 2012 to be sold to Remy Cointreau at £58m giving the initial investors a very substantial return on their investment.

The range at Bruichladdich has been consolidated and only has 4–5 products of each of the three styles produced at the distillery. One very popular expression is produced using 100% Islay barley. Also, there is the heavily peated Port Charlotte production accounting for 40% and the Ultra heavy peated Octomore, accounting for 10% of its production. The owners are hoping to revive the traditional malting floors within the next 3–5 years.

Using a Lomond Still, affectionately known as "Ugly Betty", salvaged from Inverleven Distillery in Dumbarton, Gin is also produced here, their Botanist Gin has proved hugely popular. A recent report claimed that the revenue from the Botanist Gin outstripped the revenue from the Bruichladdich malt whisky! (Page 25 Ugly Betty)

A popular offering to visitors is the opportunity to bottle your own from two casks always available at the Visitor Centre, these casks are chosen by Distillery staff and the bottling is known as Valinch. Another popular offering is the Warehouse tasting with the opportunity to sample from three casks, one Bruichladdich, one Octomore, and one Port Charlotte.

Under Remy Cointreau, the distillery has been a member of the Scotch Whisky Association SWA since 2012.

Tour Suggestion 5:
Explore the Isle of Jura and Another Famous Distillery!

The regular vehicle ferry crosses the fast-flowing Sound of Islay for the short journey between Port Askaig on Islay to Feolin on Jura. Admire the Paps of Jura ahead and have your camera ready for the wonderful view of Islay from the sea. Disembark and begin the eight-mile road north to Craighouse and the **Isle of Jura Distillery**.

Jura is 29 miles long by 7 miles wide. The west is wild and virtually uninhabited, occupied only by the three Paps, known as The Mountain of the Sound, The Mountain of Gold, and The Sacred Mountain. (The conical shape of three hills is due to freeze/thaw action on quartz which splits into scree). The land's challenging annual Fell Race takes place on the last weekend in May.

Jura is divided into seven private estates and is famous for its Paps, deer, whisky, and George Orwell. Before he moved to Jura (1946–49), Orwell was well known for his novels *Animal Farm* and *The Road to Wigan Pier*. However, the islanders knew him by his real name, Eric Blair, where he lived an isolated existence in the north at Barnhill while working on his new novel *1984*. On one occasion he and his young son almost lost their lives when rowing a dinghy through the notorious Corryvrecken whirlpool, fortunately, they were spotted and saved by a lobster fisherman. Sadly, Orwell's health deteriorated and, in 1949, he left Jura for London where he died of TB aged only 46.

Approximately one mile past the main settlement of Craighouse is the ancient burial ground of St Earnadail. One grave slab is particularly interesting, Mary McCrain who died aged 128, and Gillour McCrain who, allegedly spent 180 Christmases in his own home! The probable explanation is that Jura recognised the old and new calendar, so old and new would both have been celebrated. The calendar officially changed in 1790.

You are almost guaranteed to spot Red Deer on Jura and these are considered relatively "purebred" as they are not tainted by interbreeding with non-native Sika deer which happens elsewhere on the mainland.

Jura has a population of about 190 but this number was boosted recently by the arrival of contractors to work on the Ardfin Estate and Jura House. New owner Greg Coffey has invested £50m to develop a world-class golf club. A total renovation of Jura House and redundant farm buildings took place to create luxury accommodation. Jura House was originally built in the 18th C by the Campbells of Jura. Sydney-born Mr Coffey retired recently after making £430m from trading deals.

Isle of Jura Distillery (Deer Island)

Founded 1810, closed 1913, rebuilt 1958–1963 by the well-known 20th C Distillery architect, William Delme-Evans, a Welshman with French blood, he championed an up-to-date Gravity flow distillery design which improved efficiency. He also built the airstrip on Jura, obtained a flying license, and bought a small Cessna 172 airplane. This enabled him to commute easily from his Hertfordshire home to the Isle of Jura, he also served as the Distillery Manager until 1975. However, the illegal distillation of whisky had been ongoing for many years previously in a cave close to the present distillery.

This distillery is not classed as an Islay Distillery but it must qualify as one of the top five most remote in Scotland! You can only reach it via the small Islay to Jura ferry followed by a single-track road from the ferry port, this is probably why most visitors to Islay distilleries never make it to Jura. Don't make this mistake it is well worth the small effort. (Page 26 Jura)

The distillery is owned by Whyte & Mackay, which in turn is owned by the Emperador group, headquartered in Manila.

Capacity is 2.4 million litres of spirit per year, the distillery style is non-peated Highland whisky, except for four weeks each year when a heavily peated spirit is produced at 45ppm. This Jura Malt has experienced an incredible growth in sales, up 150% in the last decade, and is now selling 1.7 million bottles worldwide, quite an achievement for a remote distillery on a sparsely populated island.

The owners have begun upgrading the visitor centre provision within their group's portfolio distilleries and perhaps Jura will be next.

In 2018 the whole range was discontinued and replaced by new bottlings. One is called Seven Wood (a vatting of whiskies matured in seven types of wood, first Bourbon and then a finish in each of Vosges, Jupilles, Les Bertranges, Allier, Tronçais, and Limousin casks), the result is spicy with overtones of chocolate and fruit. Their duty-free range names are inspired by local landmarks, e.g. The Sound, The Road, The Loch, and The Paps. Unfortunately, the popular "Prophecy" bottling was discontinued. The name recalled a well-known Jura story about a prophecy that came true and related to the departure of the last Campbell of Jura. The full story is on display just outside the distillery.

Food and refreshments are available next door at the Isle of Jura Hotel.Gin anyone?

If you fancy sampling another local Spirit, then continue driving northwards towards the Ardlussa Estate, where, in 2015, three entrepreneurial women joined forces and produced the highly recommended Lussa Gin using local botanicals.

Tour Suggestion 6:
Explore the Isle of Colonsay

The Isle of Colonsay and More Gin

A day trip from Port Ellen on Islay to Colonsay takes 70 mins on the ferry. www.calmac.co.uk

(Strand)

Colonsay has beautiful beaches, wonderful coastal scenery, birdlife, feral goats, and fascinating archaeology.

There is also a golf course, book shop, an excellent microbrewery, and the new Colonsay Gin Distillery is a welcome addition to the island.

Excellent food and local produce are available in The Pantry, close to the ferry port at Scalasaig.

Macphie Bagging: There are 22 hills over 300 feet (aka Macphies) attracting hikers and fitness fanatics to scale each one.

The Isle of Colonsay is the ancestral land of Clan Macphie (aka MacDuffie). From the 1200s the clan occupied a hillfort at Dun Eibhinn and buried their dead on nearby Oransay, their clansmen/women are now scattered worldwide.

Archaeology: In 1995 a small hill was excavated on the east coast at Staosnaig, it was found to be a midden pit, or ancient rubbish dump, with hundreds of thousands of hazelnut shells. Evidence of roasting the nuts was also found in adjoining pits. These dated from the Mesolithic period (c9,000 years ago) when the first colonisers after the Ice Age were travelling around the landscape exploiting natural resources. At harvest time many hands would have been required to process the nuts suggesting Colonsay was a gathering place for social interaction with other hunter-gatherer groups. The roasted and processed nuts would have been easier to transport almost like an ancient peanut butter!

Colonsay also has the highest concentration of Viking graves found anywhere in Scotland, one of the most striking was found in the sand dunes in beautiful Kiloran Bay in 1882. This area was a perfect landing spot for Viking longships. The Lords of the Isles were descended from Norse/Gael warriors, see Finlaggan on Islay. Archaeologists uncovered the remains of a man, his horse, and a range of Viking grave goods. These remains can be seen in the National Museum of Scotland in Edinburgh. This is only one of six such burials here and a further five on nearby Oransay.

Southwards, the Strand is a mile-wide sandy causeway to linking Colonsay to neighbouring Oransay. Oransay is only accessible at low tide. Caution – don't cross without knowing tidal times or you risk being stranded!

Meanwhile Back on ISLAY – Much more to see and do.

Tour Suggestion 7:
Coastal Day Tour from
Bowmore towards the Rhinns

Westwards on A847 towards Bruichladdich and arrive at Port Charlotte.

Port Charlotte

This is the cultural centre of Islay. Port Charlotte was founded in 1828 by Colin Campbell for the distillery workers at Lochindaal Distillery. The town was named for his mother and each house measures exactly the same. The distillery closed in 1929 but some buildings still remain, one old warehouse houses the Wildlife Information Centre. Recently there was talk that Bruichladdich had plans to reopen, but to date, no more information is available.

Housed inside the old Church, opposite the Rhinns Medical Centre, is the excellent Museum of Islay Life. Inside are a range of interesting exhibits relating to Islay life including an illicit Still. Some fascinating carved stones can also be seen here.

The Port Charlotte hotel features regular live music sessions, good pub food, and a wide range of Islay Malts.

(Portnahaven)

Continue on the A847 towards picturesque **Portnahaven** and neighbouring **Port Wemyss,** tranquil villages overlooking the sea. You're almost certain to spot seals basking on the shoreline here.

This pretty village, built-in 19th C, was mainly for fishing and crofting. There is no distillery, hence the main road has not been improved!

Look for the local Church which boasts two entrances. It was designed to serve two different local communities hence each was given its own separate entrance.

In the 1820s, Scottish engineer, Thomas Telford, was commissioned to build 32 standard churches with manse and byre throughout the Highlands and Islands of Scotland. He had a strict budget to adhere to. However, parishioners here raised a little extra to install a gallery inside.

On a wall by the Church is an OK corner, a popular meeting place for youngsters (meet you at the corner, OK?)

There is a good pub by the harbour for refreshment and the Rhinns Lighthouse (1825) was built by Robert Stevenson, a member of the famous Stevenson family of Lighthouse Builders.

(Claddich)

Further around the coast (SW) is a pretty sandy bay at Claddach.

Offshore, at the extreme SW is the rocky outcrop known as Frenchman's Rocks. This is a popular place for bird watchers. Autumn is the best time for spotting sea birds, shearwaters, petrels, gannets, and auks.

Continue your journey northwards on the narrow road towards **Kilchiaran** (9 miles) founded by St Columba in memory of his tutor who died in 548AD.

Before you reach Kilchiaran, look out for a Stone circle at Cultoon on the left. There are some large boulders at the entrance to a field just beyond the gate. Do not park here and climb over the gate! Drive on, stop at layby then walk to the stones.

A little further on you will see an early farm, D-shaped with the water mill and ancillary farm buildings, these date from 1826. This is an interesting example of agricultural improvements when new farming methods were introduced following the harsh eviction of tenant farmers.

Offshore are the dangerous reefs where many ships were wrecked. Two troopships during World War I and, earlier in 1859, the Mary Ann of Greenock was wrecked.

Arriving at Kilchoman, once the most populated part of Islay due to the productiveness of the land, is the ruined Church dedicated to St Comman who was associated with the Holy Island of Iona on Scotland's west coast. The High Cross is much earlier dating from the 1300s. This has been a religious site and settlement for many centuries, the current Church being built on the same spot as numerous predecessors. A number of interesting medieval grave slabs can be seen alongside. The Church is now in a very poor state of repair so please don't enter. However, on the plus side, look out for the rare Choughs who nest in the roof timbers, you may see them flying in and out at certain times of the year.

This area, overlooking the bay, was the summer residence of the Lords of the Isles where their dogs were trained to hunt for seals.

Close by and a short walk is the Kilchoman Military Cemetery, follow the main road and turn left by Coastguard Cottages. At the highest point of the graveyard lie 70 'Otranto' victims who lost their lives in 1918. This area is popular with photographers because of the wonderful sunsets. Go eastwards to return to Bowmore.

Tour Suggestion 8:
From Bowmore South to the Oa

Leaving Bowmore, aim south towards Port Ellen and follow signs to An Oa (pronounced Oh) passing Kilnaughton Chapel and cemetery with a wonderful view to Carraig Fhada Lighthouse by the singing sands. Why not try the singing sands for yourself? Enjoy a stroll on the beach and gently move your feet over the sand and listen.

On a clear day, the views are stunning, you can even see the coast of Northern Ireland to the southwest.

The ruins of 15th C, some parts are probably of an earlier date, Kilnaughton Chapel (*Church of St Nechtan*[7]) features some interesting medieval grave slaps including a West Highland Warrior in full armour.

The population who lived around here during the 1800s mostly left for Canada but many were also attracted by the growing industries in Glasgow. They were not forcibly or brutally evicted as was common in other parts of Scotland but they were 'encouraged' to leave by their misguided landlords. This area became devoid of people and filled with sheep. Islay's population in the mid 19th C is thought to have been up

---

[7] St Nechtan c 7th C Saint

to 10,000 and ruined croft houses are a common sight throughout the island.

A short walk, about one mile, from the car park takes you to the American Monument. In 1918, 266 American servicemen lost their lives when their troopship (SS Tuscania) was sunk by German U boats just off Islay's coastline. 132 made it to shore, many with nasty injuries having been forced against rocks by the tide. Many corpses were found washed up on the beach in the following days and sadly many bodies were never recovered. Burials took place throughout the island and some were laid to rest in the Graveyard by Kilnaughton Chapel. Local women brought pieces of red white and blue material to make a US flag[8] for the burials. The high number of casualties shocked the US nation and received widespread throughout the country.

In October the same year, barely a month before Armistice, yet another troop carrier 'HMS Otranto' suffered a collision during a heavy storm with reported 40ft waves resulting in the tragic loss of a further 431 US lives.

The area around the Monument is an RSPB Reserve with a car park. Bird-friendly farming methods are used here too, including out-wintering of cattle to produce insect-rich dung essential for feeding certain species. Reed buntings, twite, thrush, and linnets are helped by the traditional method of cropping oats and barley and leaving the winter stubble.

---

[8] The flag was sewn overnight in time for the first funeral to take place. The flag was later sent to the US where it is displayed in the Smithsonian National Museum in Washington DC.

Statistics

Good to Know:

All figures relate to Jan-Dec 2019 unless stated.
www.scotch-whisky.org.uk

- PPM – One ppm is equivalent to the absolute fractional amount multiplied by one million.
- Islay at full production has the capacity to produce **23m** litres of spirit alcohol per year.
- **42** bottles (70cl @40% ABV) of Scotch Whisky are shipped from Scotland to **175** markets around the world each second, totalling over **1.3bn** ever.
- Laid end to end those bottles would stretch about **350,000kms** – that's 90% of the distance to the moon!
- Scotch Whisky exports are worth **£4.9bn.**
- In 2018, Scotch Whisky accounted for **75%** of Scottish food and drink exports, **21%** of all UK food and drink exports, and **1.3%** of all UK exports.
- The Scotch Whisky industry provides **£5.5bn** in gross value added (GVA) to the UK economy.
- More than **10,000** people are directly employed in the Scotch Whisky industry in Scotland and over **40,000** jobs across the UK are supported by the industry.
- **7,000** of these jobs in rural areas of Scotland providing vital employment and investment to communities across the Highlands and Islands.
- There are **2 million** visits to Scotch Whisky distilleries a year, making the industry the third most popular tourist attraction in Scotland.

- Some **20 million** casks lie maturing in warehouses in Scotland waiting to be discovered.

- To be called Scotch Whisky, the spirit must mature in oak casks in Scotland for at least **three** years.

- There are currently **133** operating Scotch Whisky distilleries across Scotland.

- "The Angels Share" refers to the amount of whisky lost to evaporation. While whisky is 'sleeping' in casks up to 2% can be lost to the atmosphere, this is "The Angels Share".

© Maggie McLeod

Printed in May 2023
by Rotomail Italia S.p.A., Vignate (MI) - Italy